How to Write and

Publish Your Book in

30 Days

I0160717

"For many years you have been carrying around a book in you but you have not allowed it to come forth. It's time for you to deliver that book to the world and allow it to be a blessing and minister to other people. It's time for you to come out of your comfort zone and break free from the fear and uncertainty that's holding you back."

Dexter L. Jones

UWriteit Publishing Company
Goldsboro, NC USA
www.uwriteitpublishingcompany.com

This publication is designed to provide information in regard to
the subject matter covered. It is published with the
understanding that the author is not engaged in rendering legal
counsel or other professional services. If legal advice or other
professional advice is required, the services of a professional
person should be sought.

Printed in the U.S.A.

Dedication

*I dedicate this book to **God** for blessing me with the ability to write books that has been a blessing to many individuals. Also, for blessing me with the gift of Administration to become an Entrepreneur and start a publishing company that has already helped writers become present day authors.*

*I dedicate this book to my Precious wife, **Princess Petula**. I thank God for giving me a virtuous woman that loves God first and foremost. I thank God for giving me a Partner in life and in business and thank you for allowing me to do the things that God have put in my heart to do. I Love You!*

*This book is also dedicated to **all** that has a book in them but has not yet taken that step of faith to take the necessary actions to join the rank of a present day author. You are one step away from the manifestation of your book within the next 30 days.*

*Also I dedicate this book to my beautiful and precious daughter **Jasmine Shonte' Jones** a daughter that I am so proud of that brings me constant happiness. Jasmine, you have now become a present day author by co-authoring your first book at the age of 16, much success on your first book as you go forth to making it a bestseller. Much Love*

Stories of Unpublished Writers -- Now Present Day Authors

An older man for many years had the dream of putting his preached message in book form, yet at his age he had no knowledge of computers or how to prepare a manuscript in Microsoft Word. His dream of book publication for his messages seemed hopeless, what publisher would take his notes and formulate it into a book in this 21st century? Today he is a published author with two books under his belt and a third about to go into production because he found the right publisher that would take his notes and produce a book.

A young lady that has an incredible testimony and to hear it you would think that she should not even be here today. She had the dream of becoming a published author by publishing her poems. But not knowing much about the publishing industry her dreams of becoming a published author were almost up in smoke until she found the right publisher that would steer her toward the journey of manuscript preparation so that her dream could become a reality. Today, she is a published author, going forth doing speaking engagements and selling her book that is making an impact on the lives of others.

A young man in his 20's had been writing poetry for years and had many great poems he wanted to publish as a book. One morning on the way home, he was involved in a car accident that left him paralyzed and his hands almost immobile. His dream of being an author was almost shattered. He was determined to see his poems in print and he completed his manuscript with his bare knuckles typing it out on his computer. Today he is a published author, doing speaking engagements and working on his second book. He also found the right publisher that was willing to help make his dream come true.

These individuals are no different than you, they had the desire to become a present day author and see their work in print and making an impact in the lives of others. If you're ready to publish your book then you hold within your hand the material that will show you how to write and publish it within the next 30 days. The procrastination stops today, get rid of the slothfulness and get ready for a new mindset that will equip you to become a present day published author. No matter what challenges and obstacles have held you back get ready for the dawning of a new day. You hold within your hands the secrets that will take you from a procrastinator to a writer and from a writer to a published author. That book that should have been written years ago we will show you how to get it published within the next 30 days. Get ready for a journey of inspiration, motivation and change that will spur you on to success as an author with pride and dignity because you have accomplished a task that many desire to do but don't know where to begin or how to complete. Are you ready? Then let's begin now and I will see you in 30 days on the other side among the list of present day authors.

TABEL OF CONTENTS

Introduction

Introduction

Now is the time to write that book that you have been putting off for many years. As an author I understand what it's like to desire to get your first book published. No doubt there are many unanswered questions about getting a book published that you may be pondering at this time. Questions such as:

- How do I start writing this book?
- How do I finish up this book?
- How do I know if I'm going with the right publisher?
- Am I paying too much to get my book published?
- What about my rights to my book?
- How do I prepare a manuscript?
- How can I protect myself, I don't have my work copyrighted yet?
- How do I market and promote my book etc…?

Within this book we answer these questions and show you how to get started writing that book or complete the book you started on. This is the book that will show you how to get from where you are to where you want to be, a published author.

However, I also know what it's like to see your book finally published and you holding that finished book in your hand. There is also a feeling that derives from within when that book has touched people's lives and inspired, motivated and encouraged your readers.

I've truly been blessed as an author to write so many books that has touched the lives of many individuals, now it's our mission to help empower you to enjoy that same feeling of accomplishment. I pray that the following pages will inspire and inform you to begin writing now. Here is your road map and guide to direct your path from the life of a writer to the life of a publisher author. We wish you much success as a published author and we welcome you to join the ranks of those who have fulfilled their lifelong dream of seeing their work in print.

UWriteIt Publishing Company
Dexter & Petula Jones

1

Your Mind is the Battlefield

"The mind is your battlefield, decisions and choices are won and made within the mind and we see the outcome of your choices manifested in your daily life."

The one idea I want to convey to you in this chapter relates to the thoughts in your mind on a daily basis. As a society we have failed to realize the power of our thoughts, we've failed to realize that the thoughts which dominate our thinking has a direct correlation and connection with the things that we experience in our life. Here are six of the most powerful words that I can relate to you that can change your life as a writer.

WE BECOME WHAT WE THINK ABOUT

Where you are right now as a writer is a result of the thoughts that continually dominate your thinking.

- *You cannot wish, hope and desire to write that book that you've always wanted to write and then have negative thoughts of failure and procrastination dominating your thought life.*

- *Either one thought pattern or the other will*

dominate your mind and produce results in accordance with the dominating thoughts you're thinking.

- *You can't think one way and then expect another way to come forth, the thoughts you're sowing in your mind you will reap in your life and there's no way around it. You will become what you think.*

- *You must come to the knowledge that your thoughts are what you and your life as a writer will become. There is no exception to this rule you will become the dominating thoughts that you're thinking.*

There is a universal law in the realm of the mind that works the same for all mankind and that law is; **"like attract like, cause and effect, what you sow, you will reap, and everything produces after its kind."** An apple tree cannot produce oranges nor can a pecan tree produce plums every tree produces after its kind. Therefore, you must begin to renew your mind.

- *Your thinking needs to change from failure consciousness to "success consciousness."*

- *Your thinking needs to change from I'll never get this book written to "I will have this book written within the next 30 days."*

- **Your thinking needs to change from I don't have enough time to write to** *"I will make time to write this book.*

- **Your thinking needs to change from no one will buy this book to** *"I will sell my book and promote it to become a bestseller."*

- **Your thinking needs to change from I can't to"** *I can do all things through Christ which strengths me."*

And when you change your thoughts your whole life change. Your thoughts create your circumstances and lifestyle. Your thoughts create images and the image that you consistently hold in your mind will produce for you according to the image of that thought.

Man is not a creature of conditions but instead creates his conditions by his dominating thoughts. In essence, what you think you will soon become and as you continue to think so you continue to be. The dominating thoughts of your mind that's hidden from others will attract to you the environment and circumstance which your thoughts secretly longs for whether good or bad. We know what you're thinking by the circumstance and situations that surround your life, if you're dissatisfied with the picture your life is portraying as a writer to yourself and others then change it by simply changing your thinking.

Begin to see yourself not as you are but visualize (or form a mental image of) yourself as if you were what you want to be, a published author.

2

Begin to Write Now

Write your first sentence and your sentences will turn into a paragraph and your paragraphs will turn into a chapter and your chapters will turn into a book. But until you begin to write that first sentence your book will never see the light of day. Writers are notorious procrastinators and you have probably already put off writing your book and getting it published for many years. You may even have written a chapter or two but your lack of persistence has caused you to put it aside and neglect finishing your book.

From this day forward you must begin to write now. No more excuses you have made all kinds of excuses for your slothfulness and neglect. But until you begin to write now you will not become a published author. You will spend the rest of your days regretting that you did not write that book that you always wanted to write and should have written. Some of the saddest words in the English language is **"I Should Have."** What you must understand is that no one will make or force you to write that book you must get enough fortitude and persistence to do it on your own. No magic wand will come down and inspire you to make it happen, you must make it happen yourself.

Begin today to set some time aside to write that first sentence so that your creative juices can begin to flow. That first sentence will inspire the next sentence and that sentence will inspire the next sentence and that sentence will inspire the next sentence until you have written your first paragraph. After you have written your first paragraph for the day you can put your writing aside for the day or continue if you're inspired to go further. Whatever you decide you have taken the most significant step and that is you have begun to write.

Most individuals are defeated because of the simple truth that they will never begin the process of starting.

- How can you finish if you never start?
- How can you complete a project if you never begin the project?
- How can you say you have faith if you put no works behind your belief?
- How can you become a published author if you never start writing your book?
- How can you fulfill your lifelong dream if you just continue to dream about it and not make it a reality in your life?

For many years you have been carrying around a book in you but you have not allowed it to come into fruition. It's time for you to deliver that book to the world and allow it to be a blessing and minister to other people. It's time for you to come out of your comfort zone and break free from the fear and uncertainty that's holding you back.

Don't be afraid to take risk and try something new. Be bold and bring forth the gift and talent that God has placed within you. The idea of becoming a published author is definitely within the reach of every individual today. Many would be authors started out right where you are today. Having a desire to write a book but not knowing what to do or how to do it. The first step with anything is always the toughest but that first step is the starting point of all achievements. That first step is to begin and after that step is taken the second step is always easier. Most individuals are defeated as a writer simply because they will not begin. When it comes to becoming a published author how does it all begin? The process is simple and you've heard it already before.

Write your first sentence and your sentences will turn into a paragraph and your paragraphs will turn into a chapter and your chapters will turn into a book. BEGIN TO WRITE NOW!!!

3

The Manuscript

First, decide what type of book manuscript you will write: Will you write a work of non-fiction, creative non-fiction, fiction, motivation, biography, poetry, inspiration, short stories, Christian book, children book or some other type of book.

A manuscript is the original text or information of an author's work written (however publishers don't receive written submissions today) or typed out and submitted to a publisher. It's the book that you've written or typed out in the form that is received by a publisher for the publishing of the book. With the technology available today the number one form of submission that is accepted by the majority of publishers is that your work be submitted in Microsoft Word format. If you have pictures they will need to be submitted mainly in jpeg format.

We are of the belief that every person has at least one book inside of them. In reality, many people dream of writing a book, but few take the necessary steps essential to fulfill their dream. When you begin to write your book it can be an awesome experience, but it's also one of the greatest challenges you will experience. Writing a manuscript takes dedication and persistence to not just start but to see the job through to the end. Many individuals start out with great hopes and dreams but somewhere along the way they lose their focus, zeal and enthusiasm and their interest and devotion came to a halt.

Our objective in this section is to inspire you to not only start your manuscript but to complete it unto the end. We will show you how easy it is to actually fulfill your mission of finishing your manuscript and making it ready for the publisher. Here are some ideas that will help you as you prepare your manuscript for publication.

1. Decide on the best time that you can set aside to begin writing or completing your manuscript. This must be a time that you can work without interruption.

2. Come up with different ideas for your book, and choose the one you like best.

3. Set goals for accomplishing your book manuscript so that you will have daily achievements that you are making towards writing or finishing your book. Writers are notorious for procrastinating, so consider setting writing goals for yourself: For example, set a goal to write 1,000 words a day, 20 pages a week or whatever works best for your schedule. (We will talk more about this later).

4. Do research for your book if it requires having accurate facts or statistics. There are many ways of doing research today and the

most common way is of course online research. However, don't forget your local library it has a wealth of information there.

5. A good method for writing your book is to prepare an outline for your book. However, some individuals prefer not to start with an outline but to write as the information or message comes to them. An outline can be a great method because it helps you to know where your book is going and the path that you're taking to get there. However, whatever method works best for you.

6. Whatever you do you must at some point begin to write. That manuscript will not write itself you must decide how you will get started and by what method, but the beginning of that manuscript will begin with you writing that first sentence. Don't worry about making the book perfect, as you go along you can come back later and edit it and make all other corrections, but begin now.

7. Once you have written your manuscript put it aside for awhile and then come back in a couple of days and read it over again. By doing this it will enable you to come back at a

later date and view it from a fresher and different perspective.

8. Before you send in your manuscript to the publisher make sure that you have edited it as perfect as possible. Some print on demand publishers will print your book as you give it to them without much editing at all. We have seen books done by big print on demand publishing companies that were horrific. But what the author fails to realize is that the book which they send to the publisher is pretty much printed as is. So we encourage you to edit, edit, edit your manuscript for typos, grammar and misspelled words. I have yet to see a perfect book but you want it as perfect as possible.

9. Different publishers have different requirements even though there are many similarities with all publishers. Whichever publisher you decide make sure to find out all the submission requirements you will have to meet.

10. Before you submit your manuscript make sure that you have thoroughly gone through it before you submit it to the publisher.

The Mind of a Winner

"Within the mind of a winner is the attitude of gratitude and the belief that they win in life because winning is all about attitude."

To be a true winner in life you must have the mind of a winner. The winner's mind is a mind that is focused on its objective and will persist until it fulfills its mission. Only by having a focused mind can you change your life from that of a dreamer to that of a published author? Throughout this book we will give you a simple and easy to understand formula that will help you to write or finish that book within the next 30 days. All you have to do is follow the formula that we will lay out for you and you will begin a process of eliminating excuses and the many reasons why you can't complete your book and begin attracting to your life the attitude that wins and the knowhow to complete your manuscript in the next 30 days. This process will enable you to get rid of:

1. **Excuses**
2. **Negative attitudes**
3. **Procrastination**
4. **Slothfulness**
5. **Inaction**
6. **Idleness**
7. **Doubt and unbelief**

The basis of making anything happen for you and turning things around in your life is belief.

- **Belief is enough to change any situation.**
- **Belief can enable you to excel in your writing.**
- **Belief can turn bad into good.**
- **Belief is the answer to you excelling as an author.**
- **Belief is the answer to making you feel like a winner.**
- **Belief is the trampoline that can bounce you into the destiny of a published author.**
- **Belief is the answer to enabling you to resist procrastination and slothfulness.**
- **Belief can do a thousand other things too numerous to mention.**

You are where you are at this very moment because of your belief system that you have held in your mind about starting or finishing that manuscript. The reason that you haven't written and published that book is because of the belief system and the thoughts that dominate your thinking. But beliefs can change from what it is to what you want it to be. You are the recipient of the strong beliefs that are now dominant in your heart. Change your belief and you change your life. If you've always had problems believing, fear not for what you will learn throughout this book is a very powerful formula and it will cause your belief to grow strong and your belief will in return do for you whatever you need it to do.

Belief is one of the laws of Absolutes. An absolute is something which is complete, correct, pure and right. When properly conformed to the law of absolutes will never let you down. However, if you violate the law of absolutes two things will manifest in life. Either you will experience from minor injury to complete chaos occurring. Also, the thing about the law of absolutes is that it is inviolable and self-enforcing, in other words it has a mind of its own and when it's violated it moves into action.

However, when it's obeyed it likewise moves into action to bring forth success and achievement. In life this law works with absolute certainty and infallibility. There is not a person on the face of the earth that the law of absolutes is not working for right now. In your life as a writer if you're experiencing more failure than success, more bad than good and making more wrong decisions than right decisions, this means that you have violated the belief law of absolutes and it is working against you as a writer at this very moment instead of for you. But we have the remedy that will change all that and will get you on the side of the law of absolutes that will work for you without fail. All you have to do is follow the formula for the next 30 days and watch that book that you formerly have had so much trouble writing or finishing, you will complete it in record time. If you're tired of:

- **Being unable to excel as a writer and always coming up with excuses.**

- **Feeling like a loser as a writer.**

- **Being unfocused.**

- **Being controlled by procrastination and slothfulness in your life as a writer.**

- **Being on a course that seems to always leave you with an unfinished manuscript.**

- **And not even fulfilling promises that you make to yourself about your book.**

Then this book is the right source of information to change all that and begin your life as a writer anew. There is only one need and that is to confess this phrase twice a day for the next 30 days as you go forth to write and complete your manuscript. You will need to confess the phrase in the morning when you arise and at night right before you go off to sleep. You can even confess it throughout the day as an added benefit. As you confess the phrase confess it boldly with feelings and conviction. These words will begin to change your thinking and create dominating thoughts that will create circumstances and situations that are relevant to your confession.

Begin to see yourself not as you are but visualize yourself as if you were what you want to become, you can do this through meditation.

Here is what to do to complete that manuscript: Go into a quite place and begin to meditate on the phrase you will see below. The term mediation is defined as: to ponder over, to think and reflect upon. It means to take these words and turn them over in your mind and to say them out so that you can hear them.

Here is the phrase that you will say for the next 30 days, **"I am completing my manuscript and every day in every way I am getting better and better."**

These words will have a powerful effect on your mind and your spirit. Likewise, see yourself in your imagination finishing your manuscript. See yourself rejoicing because you have finally done what have taken you years to accomplish and you have done it in 30 days.

Imagine it in detail, see the surroundings, feel it, smell it, touch it, hear it, let it be so real that you can taste its outcome. Begin this exercises twice daily, watch the effects of what is happening in your life as a writer, you will begin to notice changes, extraordinary accomplishments, great self-esteem, action, new ideas, awareness, productivity and ambition. These are the changes that are evolving you into the mind of a winner.

Are you up for the challenge?

Do you want to change your life as a writer to become a published author bad enough to do this? Want is vital to achieving this and faith without works is dead. You activate your faith by doing it and you prove you want it by following the formula. This is the first part of the formula for your writing success. If you will do this faithfully you will form a mindset that will lead you on to victory as a writer. No more:

- Excuses
- Procrastination
- Slothfulness
- Indecisiveness
- Inaction

Now is the time to get that book written and make it available to the world. Follow this first formula to the letter for the next thirty days and your manuscript will see the light of day and before you know it you will be holding your very own book in your hand and will be acclaimed a published author.

If you're ready, let's get started with the second part of the formula that will enable you to not only get started on your manuscript but will equip you to get it done now.

4

Set a Daily Goal

If you're ready, let's get started with the second part of the formula, the difference that makes the difference. Most writers fail right here because they fail to set daily goals.

If you are to become a published author you must begin to write now. I know that we are overemphasizing and reiterating this point but we must in order to drive it home and cause you to take action. One thing that will help you start or finish that manuscript is that you must begin to set a daily goal to write. Goals are not a bad thing but a goal is the number one avenue that will enable you to get the work done. Without a goal you will simply drift from day to day, week to week, month to month and year to year without accomplishing anything. Goals are essential for achievement. A writer without goals will not get much done and will find that their life as a writer has passed them by and that book that was supposed to be written years ago is still nothing but a dream and a thought.

You must choose whether you want to become a published author or are you just speaking vain words that have no real substance. I want to get tough with you for a moment because obviously up to this point in your life no one has confronted you about your writing.

- Are you truly a writer or just a dreamer?

- Do you truly have what it takes or no?

- Will you be beaten by procrastination or will you suck it up and begin to write?

- Will you stop making excuses or will you begin to plan and prepare yourself to become that published author?

- Is this just another venture of yours or are you ready to become a winning author?

If you want something that you've never had then you must do something that you've never done. If you keep repeating the same process you will keep getting the same results. You can't expect different results following the same pattern.

If you want different results than what you've had in the past as a writer then you must choose a different course of action for the future. It's all in the power of choice.

You're where you are today as a result of the choices you made in the past as a writer. That manuscript is not done because you allowed inaction, things, excuses, slothfulness and procrastination to dominate your choices. Well, no more, today is the turning point in your life and 30 days from now you will be the new author that will be added to the list of present day published authors.

THINKING FOR A CHANGE

At any time, you can change any of the choices you've made in the past as a writer and the change will produce for you a different set of results.

- You are not bound to the life you're currently experiencing as a writer, if you're unhappy you can change it by simply choosing a different course of action.

- If you're not happy being an unpublished author, you can change it if you're willing to make both mental and natural changes.

- If the course of action you're currently following isn't bringing you closer to your goal as a published author then you need to do something different than what you're currently doing.

- You can't keep doing business the same old way and expect different results.

Taking a different course of action doesn't have to be anything drastic but it must be something different than what you're doing now.

As an example let us observe one idea that can make all the difference. If you having been trying to start or finish up your manuscript but have not been successful you must begin to take a different course of action to accomplish your goal. That course of actions can be something as simple as setting a daily goal to write a certain amount of words or pages each and every day.

Set goals, so your dream of writing a book manuscript actually becomes a reality. Writers are notorious for procrastinating, so consider setting writing goals for yourself: For example, set a goal to write 1,000 words a day, 20 pages a week or whatever works best for your schedule. The key is you must set some goal or you will find yourself accomplishing little or nothing.

Let's say your book is 70 pages, if you were to write 23.5 pages a week for the next three weeks you will have your book finished in three weeks time. That calculates to writing about three and a half pages a day or 1000 words a day. If you want to stretch it out to the full four weeks then you will have to write only 17 pages a week or 825 words a day. Of course if you book is smaller or larger then the pages per week and the words per day will be different.

Now that you have a formula and a pattern to write there is no more excuses why you cannot get that manuscript done. Do it now! Watch what happens when you take action and do it now, excuses, procrastination and slothfulness goes out the door and flee from your life like a bird that has been set free from a trap. You can set aside a couple of hours a day to write in order to start or finish up your manuscript. That time will be your writing time, you will choose a place and time that you can go without interruption or distractions. Your mind may try to come up with excuses why you do not have a couple of hours a day, but I say that's a bunch of bologna. You have time, let me show you some of the time that you have and what you need to do.

- You watch television for hours a day, cut out some of that time for writing.
- You may talk on the phone for hours a day, cut out some of that time for writing.
- You may just be out doing nonessential things that you don't have to do, cut out some of that time for writing.

You have 24 hours in a day just like everyone else, eight of those hours are for sleeping, eight are for working and you have eight to do whatever else you want to do. Now the question is what are you doing with those eight discretionary hours that you have? Most people are doing one of the three things mentioned above and neither one is helping them accomplish their goals as a writer or author.

In conclusion it all boils down to choices. The right choices will lead you on to success as a writer and the wrong choices will contain you as you are a dreamer and an unfulfilled writer.

- *The right choices are the driving force in the life of the lifeless.*

- *The right choices are the power that will strengthen the weak and aimless.*

- *The right choices empower you with authority that gives you the permission to succeed in life as a writer.*

- *The right choices empower you with influence that gives you the confidence to go boldly after your life's goal of becoming a published author.*

- *The right choices will produce for you the life and blessings of a present day author.*

Your life consists of choices and you have the God-given ability within you to make right choices and become all that God has designed for you in life as a writer and author. Will you do it or will you not, it's your choice?

5

Marketing and Promoting Your Book

"Marketing is not always easy but it's essential in order to let the world know that your book is now available."

Now that you have written your manuscript and it is sent to the publisher the hat that you must put on now, is the hat of the marketer and promoter of your book. Actually, you can start marketing and promoting your book even before you finish it when your mindset is changed into that of a doer and you know that your book will be done.

Marketing is an essential part of making your book known to the world. Marketing is also the method that will help you to reach your goal of selling books. However, marketing is a subject that many writers don't like to deal with, but if you want to sell books you must know that it's a part of the author's agenda. As an author you have to promote yourself and let the world know that your book is available. Many authors don't like to do this and also many authors don't know where to start. Marketing and promoting does not have to be a difficult task but it is something that you will have to learn to do if you are not familiar with how to do it in an effective manner.

Your whole goal in marketing and promoting your book is to get it into the hands of potential readers that are looking for the kind of book that you have written. The truth is that everyone does not want your book no matter how good it is. Your book does not fit into everyone's reading category but it does fit into the category of enough people to make it a number one bestseller. Here are the ABC's of marketing:

- A = **Audience** — pick a target audience; have a preferred audience that your book reaches out to.

At my current age of 48, I have no interest in a book written that tells me about how to potty train a child. An author that will send me a flyer, email me or that will make me their target audience will simply be wasting their time and money marketing their book to me. I have no interest at all in such a book. A book about potty training a child will be better marketed to women or a couple in their early 20's to 30's and preferably to couples or an individual that are having or have their first child. That author will have a greater chance of success with those individuals buying their book than hoping that I will purchase their book.

As an author you must know the audience that you're writing to and then you must target that audience and market and promote your book to that particular audience. Here are some examples to give you some ideas:

- Books written for singles should be targeted to singles not married couples.
- Books written to married couples should be targeted mainly too married couples (some singles could benefit if they're looking to be married in the future).
- Poetry books should be targeted to those individuals that like poetry and not to everyone.
- Books on finances should be targeted mainly to individuals that want to change their financial status or need help with money management.
- Books for teens should be targeted to parents and teens.
- Books that are written directly to girls or boys should be targeted specifically to that particular audience.
- Books written about children or babies should be targeted to parents and especially new or first time parents.
- Books that are written for the Christian arena should be targeted mainly for those that are Christians.
- Books that are written about relationships should be targeted to those that have that inter-

est, mainly couples in relationship or married couples, depending on the content of the book.

- Fiction books should be targeted to those individuals that like reading novels, romance, etc...
- This is really not rocket science, you know what type of book you have written and who you've written it for, now target that particular audience.

One thing about writers that I have noticed is they believe that their book will be accepted by all and that everyone would love to read it. This is far from the truth and you will just end up wasting your marketing time and dollars. Stick to your particular audience and focus your marketing and promotion there.

- B = **Become knowledgeable** about how to reach your target audience.

Once you know exactly what type of audience you will be marketing and promoting to, start making your list that your target audience frequent and other things such as:

- The mailing or emailing lists that they're on.
- The age group of your audience.
- The type of magazines they read.
- The type of newspapers they read.

- The places which they attend.
- The radio stations they listen to.
- The stores that they shop at.
- The websites which they visit.
- The blogs that they read.
- The newsletters that they read.

All of this information gives you the necessary knowledge that you need to reach out to your target audience and hit the bull's eye with your marketing and promotion efforts. There are also other things that you can do that are free of charge that will be an asset to letting others knows that your book is now available. Avenues such as:

1. Press releases
2. Book signing at libraries
3. Author or book launch parties
4. Flyer distribution
5. Book clubs
6. Word of mouth
7. Book reviews
8. Author website--Blogging
9. Social site marketing
10. Email marketing

- C = **Contacts** that's necessary for your book success.

In any endeavor there are contacts that you will

need to make that are essential for your success and achievement. These contacts are listed as:

1. Radio stations
2. Book reviewers
3. Your local and surrounding libraries.
4. Local and surrounding television stations.
5. Family and friends
6. Your congregation members
7. Local book stores
8. Your local newspaper
9. Online discussion groups
10. Community events in your area.
11. Blogging--this is vital contact for online sells. Learn more about this online.

All of these are various ideas for marketing and promoting your book. Now that you have the proper knowledge of how to do it you see that it's not as hard as you thought. The final key is to now apply what you know and watch the results that you will achieve.

6

The Importance of a Website

Having a book without a website in this age of technology is like having a brand new car without a motor, it will look good but it can't take you where you really need to go.

The first and foremost answer is: To make yourself known as an author on the World Wide Web. Billions of people world-wide have access to the World Wide Web. As a published author your book needs to be available on your own website for your target audience to purchase. Many individuals today shop online and sending in a check or money order to purchase your book is a thing of the past. We get many orders from individuals as far as London England that has purchased our book online as a result of our website that is available on the internet. From people right in your community to individuals cross the waters you want to let them know that you are interested in serving them. If you don't, your competitors will and they will sell their books while yours remain boxed up or in storage.

The second reason for a website is: To network with other writers and potential clients. The key to business and selling is making the right connections. Successful authors know that it's not so much what you know, but who you know. When you are on the World Wide Web you are making your book known to millions of potential clients. The thing also about a website is that they never closes down like your normal brick and mortar business; it will stay open 24 hours a day, 7 days a week.

Your website is also available to not only let others know about your book but also to give a brief synopsis of your book. You can also have pertinent information available to all who want to know more. You can give them answers to questions such as:

- How can I order your book?
- What locations can I pick it up at?
- How can they contact you?
- What is the cost of quantity orders?
- Are you available for speaking engagements?
- Tell me more about you.
- And much more…

Having a website will help answer all these questions and will also give your potential clients the ability to purchase your book from the privacy of their own home. With such availability don't you think you will be able to sell more books? With a website you will be able to do it.

Here are several great reasons for a published author to have their own website.

- Your book is available to your customers 24 hours a day!
- You can serve your customers!
- You can reach a greater clientele!
- To let people know your book exist!
- To have a brief synopsis of your book!
- To reach customers that you will not reach otherwise.
- To be able to answer questions immediately.
- To stay in contact with customers worldwide.
- To get positive and negative feedback.
- To have a place where the media can reach you.
- So you can sell books even while you sleep.

With your very own website you will be able to allow customers to buy your book right online and you keep all the profits. Your website will have ecommerce where they can purchase your book and pay for it either by check or credit card. They will receive an automatic "thank you and purchase confirmation" from your website. The whole process is friendly and easy for the customers.

The third reason for a website is: You get to keep all the profits: When you sell your book(s) online there is no middleman and your website takes the orders and send you an email letting you know about the order and you simply ship it out to the customer that purchase. There is no overhead and the cost of your website can be very minimal when done with the right company. Yet, you get to keep all the profits!

The fourth reason is: You need clients to sell your book to and through the World Wide Web you have access to millions and millions of clients. Nothing can give you exposure for your book like online selling and the beauty of it is that you don't even have to go out of your own home to let your target audience know that your book is available. The only thing you will have to do is let potential clients know that your website is available and you can do this through online and offline promotion of your website.

The fifth reason is: Your website will be your 24 hours, 7 days a week open bookstore. People are online every hour of every day searching for everything from books to cars. When you have a website you will be open when other places and stores may be closed. Your website will be like having your own personal salesperson 24 hours a day selling your book(s). You can't be that!

The sixth reason is: Competition is fierce and you are not the only one that has written a book like yours. When an individual is ready to purchase a book one of the first places they will go is online to see the availability, cost and where the book can be purchased. If you're not online then you will lose that sale to another author that has a website and has made their book available on the World Wide Web. A well designed website can make you look like a Fortune Five Hundred Company even if you're selling your books from your basement.

The seventh reason is: When you have a website it makes you look like a professional and ranks you up there with the big boys even though you may be small potatoes at the beginning. Having a website gives you a corporate image and will instill confidence in your clientele to help them believe that you're an author that knows what they're doing. Your website will also allow you to reach out to more people than you will ever be able to reach out to on your own. In return this will help to establish more customers that will purchase your book and help spread the word that can quickly enable your book to be a bestseller.

When you get ready for someone to design your website, make sure that you get a company that will not charge you an arm and a leg. There are companies that will charge you all kinds of monthly fees that can go into thousands of dollars a year. It has often been said that it's better not to have a website than to have one that looks like it has been done by your kid or hiring someone from the local college that will make it look unprofessional. You will only get one chance when someone visits your website so you want to make sure that it's done right and you're ready for business. The internet is being searched for books and items every second of every day and many will be searching for a book just like yours, so make it available and easily accessible so that your book will be the one that will be purchased by your target audience. Here's a great website design company: www.firstclasswebsite.com.

7

The Right Publisher

"Now that you've written the book the final step is to get the right publisher that will publish it for you both economically and in record time."

Picking a publisher is the final vital step to becoming a published author. However, you don't want to pick just any publisher, you want to pick a publisher that is both professional and economical. With some companies you will find a publisher that is professional but not very economical. With others you will find a company that is economical but not very professional. Getting the right publisher that is both economical and professional is truly a task in itself but there is some that are available.

One of the things you want to consider with a publisher is: Will they publish me a professional book that is store ready? Many publishers that new authors deal with mainly are defined as Print-on-Demand Publishers. These types of publishing companies are designed to print your book just as you give it to them with little or no editing. Also, they will print only the number of books that you need at a given time. With a print-on-demand publishing company you can order from 1 to 1000 books or more on demand. Gone are the days where you have to buy a minimum of 1000 books to begin with. Print-on-demand companies have really being a great asset to new authors because they have allowed you to get your book done without having to purchase a basement full of books at the beginning. This makes it more affordable for the average financially strapped writer.

However, there is a downside to all this freedom which is most of these companies will print books just like you send it to them, mistakes and all. The majority does not take the necessary time to do even an adequate job of editing and they will publish your book even if it has an abundance of misspelled words, grammatical errors, typos etc... Some will do an elementary style of editing if you pay for the additional cost to get it done. However, additional editing will drive the price up to the point where the cost is no longer economical but unaffordable for the beginning writer.

We have seen books done by big print-on-demand publishing companies that were horrific and downright shameful that they would even allow such a book to leave their press. Yet, what the new author does not understand is that these companies will do this because their title is print-on-demand and if you don't put out the additional money for a thorough editing job your book will come back to you just like you sent it to them, mistakes and all.

We've seen books that simple words were horribly misspelled throughout the book and when the author received their books they were very disappointed. However, it was too late and the author had to sell the book at cost because they were so ashamed at how the book looked.

Not only will the majority and I mean majority of print-on-demand publishing companies just print in book form what you send them but the cost can get into the thousands of dollars for few books. A lot of companies are not really concerned whether or not you sell a lot of books as long as they have their money upfront. Once they print your books and send them to you then the rest of the work is in the hands of the author. Don't be bamboozled by these companies making all kind of promises to you about your book becoming an immediate bestseller. No company can guarantee you that your book will be a bestseller; they really have no way of knowing. As a new author the most that you can hope for with a publishing company is that they will produce you a professional book at an economical price.

I have heard the stories and seen people pay to get hundreds of books done in the beginning and end up with a basement full of books that they cannot move. The author is disappointed because they thought that their book was going to immediately hit the bestseller list and they would be swept on to fame and fortune, but in the end they ended up with a financial setback and boxes full of books that they could not sell. Yet, that publishing company was smiling all the way to the bank. We want to say to all new authors and potential authors, don't be hoodwinked by publishing companies that promise much but produce little. Gone are the days for new authors where:

- A major company will be waiting just to get your manuscript in their hands.
- A major publishing company will write you out that big royalty advance check just to publish your book.
- Your dream of a book and movie deal will happen for you right after you get your first book published.

Honestly, all of these are pie-in-the-sky wishful thinking for uneducated and unknowledgeable writers. If you just want to produce a couple of books for your relatives and friends just to say that you've finally done your book and you have no dreams of grandeur then that's fine. But if you really want to see your work in stores selling, on your website selling, selling online etc… and making a difference in the lives of people then it's going to take plenty of work from you the author.

The truth of the matter is that you can make it

happen but you must make sure that your book is professionally done and that you're getting them at an economical price. We wrote this book because we have seen how so many authors have been flimflammed by publishing companies that did not deliver what the author thought they were receiving. It hurts our heart to see new authors bring their book to us because they were dissatisfied with the work of a previous publishing company and asked us if we could redo their book over. Or an author that came to us after their book was published and found out that the cost they paid to get their book done they could have gotten three times as many books done. Or even an author that had put their book(s) aside for years because they did not know how to use a computer to put their manuscript on Microsoft Word.

- What is an author to do in such cases?
- How can they trust anyone again after being burnt by a publishing company they thought they could trust?
- What are they to do if they don't know how to use a computer to put their work on the format that publishing companies require?
- How will they be able to afford to get their book published when the cost goes into the thousands of dollars?
- How will they communicate with a publisher when most of the time they cannot even get them on the phone?

As a publisher these are some of the questions and concerns that we noticed people were dealing with when they were ready to get their book published. You don't have to be one of those writers that get with the wrong publisher and later have regrets for your decision.

At the UWriteIt Publishing Company we're here to serve you as a publisher and to help make your dream come true as a writer. We have published books for many individuals from Pastors to stay at home moms and we have a list of satisfied customers. We want you to know that you don't have to put your work in the hands of a publishing company whose main objective is the bottom line. We are still writing books ourselves so we have not detached ourselves from the life of an author. We understand what you're going through and we're touched with the feelings that you feel as a writer. This is not just a business to us, this is more than a business it is a ministry and a mission.

We invite you to check out our website and view the many FAQ's that author's ask us and the credibility of our company. We will not see you as just a paycheck but we are of a kindred spirit because we're both authors and we understand that as authors we have a passion to see our work manifested in book form so that others will be inspired, motivated and encouraged as a result of the written word.

Our mission is simple **"we want to help equip you to bring your dreams to pass by being that publishing company that will publish for you a professional store ready book at an economical cost that you will be proud to call your own."** Below you will find our publishing cost for the different plans that you can choose from to get started making your dream of a writer a reality and joining the ranks of present day authors.

UWriteIt Publishing Company

Starter Plan

This plan is our most affordable plan aimed for the casual writer that wants to see his or her work in print. The Starter Plan includes all of the following: **20 paperback books**, 20-125 page book (5x8, 5.5x8.5 or 6x9 format) set-up, distribution with the purchase of an ISBN and barcode, unlimited re-prints of your book, a 15% royalty on any money received by **UWriteIt Publishing Company** for the sale of your book, limited black and white pictures, copyrighted, online distribution, 5 hours of editing of your book and $15.00 shipping for your 20 paperback books. **Cost: $265.00**

Business Plan

This plan is our business plan aimed for the somewhat serious writer that wants to distribute some of their work. The Business Plan includes all of the following: **60 paperback books**, 20-125 page book (5x8, 5.5x8.5 or 6x9 format) set-up, distribution with the purchase of an ISBN and barcode, unlimited re-prints of your book, a 25% royalty on any money received by **UWriteIt Publishing Company** for the sale of your book, limited black and white pictures throughout your book, copyright, 7 hours of editing of your book, online distribution and $30.00 shipping for your 60 paperback books. **Cost: $630.00**

Entrepreneur Plan

This plan is our Entrepreneur Plan aimed for the serious writer that is ready to make a bigger investment in their career as a writer and author. The Entrepreneur Plan includes all of the following: **125 paperback books**, 20-125 page book (5x8, 5.5x8.5 or 6x9 format) set-up, distribution with the purchase of an ISBN and barcode, unlimited re-prints of your book, a 30% royalty on any money received by **UWriteIt Publishing Company** for the sale of your book, limited black and white pictures throughout your book, copyright, 10 hours of editing of your book, online distribution, marketing and promotion of your book and $53.00 shipping for your 125 paperback books. **Cost: $1053.00**

CEO Plan

This plan is aimed at the cost efficient minded writer, who can sell many of their own copies in the marketplace. It is also aimed at the serious, career minded writer who wants to establish their name in the book industry. The CEO Plan includes all of the following with your fee: **300 paperback books**, 20-125 page book (5x8, or 6x9 format) set-up, ISBN number including barcode, full-service marketing (including 10 books sent for review with various publications), unlimited re-prints, a 35% royalty on any money received by **UWriteIt Publishing Company** for the sale of your book, limited black and white pictures, copyright, 15 hours of editing of your book, online distribution, marketing and promotion of your books and $95 shipping for your 300 paperback book. **Cost: $2065.00**

You can check out our website and see all the things we offer and other books we published at: www.uwriteitpublishingcompany.com

8

Ways to Get Money to Publish Your Book

"The person that is innovative and creative is never at the mercy of circumstances and situation."

One of the many things that hinders some writers from getting there manuscript published is their lack of money. However, you should never let money hinder your dreams of being a published author go unfulfilled. There are many ways that you can get the money to cover the cost of book publication if you're willing to be innovative and creative.

1. **Friends & Relatives** = your friends and relatives are individuals that know you and may be willing to either give towards your project or invest in it. **Example:** if you start out with the Standard Plan of publication for $280 you can gather six friends and relatives that would give or invest $50 each then you will have $300. Or you could get three people to give or invest $100 each.

2. **Pre-bought Books** = these are books that you will offer to individuals you know at a pre-discounted price. Once the books are published then you will simply deliver the pre-bought books to those that has already purchased. **Example:** if you were to sell 35 books at $12.95 that would equal out to

$453.25. You will take the cost of $280 for book publication out and still be able to order about 20 extra books.

3. **Acknowledgement Page** = this will be a page in the book where you will acknowledge the contributors or organizations by name that is willing to make a donation toward your book publication. **Example**: this will be a page in the front of the book that will list the names of your contributors or the organizations. You can get 12 contributors and/or organizations to contribute $25 each for a total of $300.

4. **Investors for Profit** = you may be able to find investors that may be willing to invest in your book for a small profit. **Example:** you can get one or more investors to invest in your book for a minimal profit that the two of you can agree on and the both of you will come out the better financially.

5. **Organization or Non-Profit** = this is an opportunity to contact your church, a business or a non-profit organization that may like to purchase books from you at a discounted price for a fund-raising project. **Example:** let's say that you contact one or two from the list above and have a minimum that must be ordered that will cover the cost of your book publication with some extra left over for additional books. If your book sells for $15.95 and you give a discount of $3.00 off with a

minimum order of 30 books you will make $388.50. The cost of the Standard Plan is $280, this will leave you a balance of $108.50, enough to get you an additional 12 books.

6. **A Mailing List** = if you have a mailing list that consist of associates, business clients, church members, classmates, etc... these are people that you could get to pre-order or contribute to your book. **Example:** contact these individuals on your mailing list and let them know about your soon coming book and see if they will be willing to pre-order or contribute to your new book.

7. **Sell Tickets** = people are always selling tickets for one thing or another, you can sell tickets for your book to your target audience of people that you may know and the winning ticket holder will receive a copy of your book. Example: if you sell the tickets for five dollars each you will need to sell 60 tickets in order to cover your book publication cost.

Whatever method you choose to raise the money to get your book published make sure that you know the exact figures you need for the total cost. We started out with the Standard Plan because it's the least expensive but you can do it with any plan, you will just need to adjust your figures.

9

Your Book Will Be Immortal And
You Will Live On

"The days of our life are numbered and we may only be here for a brief moment, but our works can live on even when we're no longer present."

As a writer the beauty of a published book is that your book will live on even after you're gone. If your book is promoted and marketed properly it could continue to bring revenues to new generations yet unborn. There is a book that was written in the 1800's by a man that has left the scene of this earthly planet but his book is yet selling today.

A book can also be a financial stream of income for generations to come for your children or relatives that will take up the torch and continue to promote it. If this is done it will keep your work alive and continue to give it the opportunity to bless a new generation of readers. All this will happen because you took the initiative to write that book so that it could be a blessing to others. You never know how your book could bless, inspire, motivate or encourage someone to make a change or difference in their life. Your book could help save a life if it is an inspirational book or it could encourage someone that needs a word of motivation.

Your book will help you to be immortal because it will cause you to live forever. When your manuscript is turned into a published book you will create something that will cause you to live on endlessly. Your book will touch others in many ways and you will be inspiring, teaching, equipping, motivating, entertaining, etc… even when you are no longer among the land of the living. Your book will continue to speak for you and will capture a new audience of people that may have never had the opportunity to meet you in person but they will meet you through your published work.

Your book will be your legacy one hundred years from now and individuals yet unborn at this time will read of you and mention your name. They will know who you are and the contribution you made to society through your published book. You will be looked at as someone of vital importance because your book will label you as an expert in the field of which you've written. Even if you've written a book of poetry you will be looked at as someone who was creative and expressed themselves through their poetry. Whatever you write you will never be looked upon the same ever again because you had the tenacity and courage to do what so many others desire but will not discipline themselves to fulfill their lifelong dream.

Welcome as you join the ranks of a present day

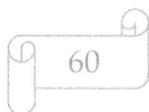

author, the world is waiting for your book and the generations yet unborn will discover it and immortalize you thereby causing you to live on forever through your published book. Thank you for taking the initial step to purchase this book but thank you more for taking the initial step to bring your book to pass so that it can bless and encourage others. We look forward to seeing your work among the present day authors.

OTHER BOOKS BY DEXTER L. JONES

1. Soul Mate or Just Another Date
2. Soul Mate or Just Another Date — Book 2
3. Soul Mates In Ministry
4. Soul Mates Bible Study & Prayer Manuel
5. Cracking the Soul Mate Code
6. Let God Help You Choose Your Husband
7. Let God Help You Choose Your Wife
8. Date Night
9. The 5 Reasons to Find Your Soul Mate and Marry
10. The 3 Greatest Myths That Keep People Single
11. Kingdom Dating
12. Kingdom Marriage
13. The Secret to Living Victorious After Your Separation or Divorce
14. The Mind of A Winner — The Teenagers Guide to Winning In Life
15. Discover Wealth Hidden In Your Salary
16. Hidden Riches of Secret Places
17. Seven Words That Will Change Your Life
18. How to Write and Publish Your Book In 30 Days
19. The Mind of A Winner — The Adult Guide to Winning In Life
20. Money Answers All Things
21. The Power of Expectation
22. And many more to come…

Some of the books were co-authored with my wife and one other was co-authored with a friend.

Dexter & Petula Jones is also available for Ministering or Speaking Engagements. We can teach on any of the topics listed in reference to the books or other topics that you may desire. We are available for seminars and workshops.

We're also available for a **"How to Write and Publish Your Book In 30 Days"** Seminar in your church, organization or corporation.

Contact us at:
www.uwriteitpublishingcompany.com
or email us at:
uwriteitpublishingcompany@yahoo.com

www.ingramcontent.com/pod-product-compliance
Lightning Source LLC
Chambersburg PA
CBHW060556100426
42742CB00013B/2585